In Loving
Memory of

_____

_____

_____

Date

Guest

Name and Address

Memory

Name and Address

Memory

_____

_____

_____

_____

_____

_____

_____

_____

_____

_____

_____

_____

_____

_____

_____

_____

_____

Name and Address

Memory

Name and Address

Memory

Name and Address

Memory

_____

_____

_____

_____

_____

_____

_____

_____

_____

_____

_____

Name and Address

Memory

Name and Address

Memory

Name and Address

Memory

Name and Address

Memory

_____

_____

_____

_____

_____

_____

_____

_____

_____

_____

_____

_____

Name and Address

Memory

_____

_____

_____

_____

_____

_____

_____

_____

_____

_____

_____

_____

_____

_____

Name and Address

Memory

_____

_____

_____

_____

_____

_____

Name and Address

Memory

Name and Address

Memory

Name and Address

Memory

Name and Address

Memory

_____

_____

_____

_____

_____

_____

_____

_____

_____

_____

_____

_____

_____

Name and Address

Memory

Name and Address

Memory

_____

_____

_____

_____

_____

_____

_____

_____

_____

_____

_____

_____

_____

_____

Name and Address

Memory

_____

_____

_____

_____

_____

_____

_____

_____

_____

_____

_____

_____

_____

_____

_____

Name and Address

Memory

_____

_____

_____

_____

_____

_____

Name and Address

Memory

_____

_____

_____

_____

_____

_____

Name and Address

Memory

_____

_____

_____

_____

_____

_____

_____

_____

_____

_____

_____

_____

_____

_____

Name and Address

Memory

_____

_____

_____

_____

_____

_____

_____

_____

_____

_____

_____

_____

_____

_____

_____

Name and Address

Memory

Name and Address

Memory

Name and Address

Memory

Name and Address

Memory

_____

_____

_____

_____

_____

_____

Name and Address

Memory

_____

_____

_____

_____

_____

_____

_____

_____

_____

_____

_____

_____

_____

_____

_____

Name and Address

Memory

_____

_____

_____

_____

_____

_____

_____

_____

_____

_____

_____

_____

_____

_____

_____

_____

Name and Address

Memory

Name and Address

Memory

_____

_____

_____

_____

_____

_____

_____

_____

_____

_____

_____

_____

Name and Address

Memory

Name and Address

Memory

Name and Address

Memory

Name and Address

Memory

_____

_____

_____

_____

_____

_____

_____

_____

_____

_____

_____

_____

_____

Name and Address

Memory

Name and Address

Memory

Name and Address

Memory

Name and Address

Memory

Name and Address

Memory

Name and Address

Memory

_____

_____

_____

_____

_____

_____

_____

_____

_____

_____

_____

_____

_____

_____

Name and Address

Memory

_____

_____

_____

_____

_____

Name and Address

Memory

Name and Address

Memory

_____

_____

_____

_____

_____

_____

Name and Address

Memory

Name and Address

Memory

_____

_____

_____

_____

_____

_____

Name and Address

Memory

Name and Address

Memory

Name and Address

Memory

Name and Address

Memory

Name and Address

Memory

Name and Address

Memory

_____

_____

_____

_____

_____

_____

Name and Address

Memory

Name and Address

_____

_____

_____

_____

_____

_____

Memory

_____

_____

_____

_____

_____

_____

_____

_____

_____

_____

Name and Address

Memory

Name and Address

Memory

_____

_____

_____

_____

_____

_____

_____

_____

_____

_____

_____

_____

_____

Name and Address

Memory

Name and Address

Memory

_____

_____

_____

_____

_____

_____

_____

_____

_____

_____

_____

_____

_____

_____

_____

_____

_____

_____

Name and Address

Memory

_____

_____

_____

_____

_____

_____

_____

_____

_____

_____

_____

_____

_____

Name and Address

Memory

_____

_____

_____

_____

_____

_____

_____

_____

_____

_____

_____

_____

_____

_____

Name and Address

Memory

Name and Address

Memory

Name and Address

Memory

Name and Address

Memory

_____

_____

_____

_____

_____

_____

Name and Address

_____

_____

_____

_____

_____

_____

Memory

_____

_____

_____

_____

_____

_____

_____

_____

_____

_____

_____

Name and Address

Memory

Name and Address

_____

_____

_____

_____

_____

_____

Memory

_____

_____

_____

_____

_____

_____

_____

_____

_____

_____

_____

Name and Address

Memory

Name and Address

Memory

Name and Address

Memory

_____

_____

_____

_____

_____

_____

_____

_____

_____

_____

_____

_____

Name and Address

_____

_____

_____

_____

_____

_____

Memory

_____

_____

_____

_____

_____

_____

_____

_____

_____

_____

_____

Name and Address

Memory

Name and Address

Memory

_____

_____

_____

_____

_____

_____

_____

_____

_____

_____

Name and Address

Memory

Name and Address

Memory

Name and Address

Memory

_____

_____

_____

_____

_____

_____

_____

_____

_____

_____

_____

_____

_____

_____

_____

_____

Name and Address

Memory

Name and Address

Memory

Name and Address

Memory

Name and Address

Memory

_____

_____

_____

_____

_____

_____

Name and Address

Memory

Name and Address

Memory

Name and Address

Memory

Name and Address

Memory

Name and Address

Memory

Name and Address

Memory

Name and Address

Memory

_____

_____

_____

_____

_____

_____

Name and Address

Memory

Name and Address

Memory

Name and Address

Memory

Name and Address

Memory

Name and Address

Memory

Name and Address

Memory

Name and Address

Memory

Name and Address

Memory

Name and Address

_____

_____

_____

_____

_____

_____

Memory

_____

_____

_____

_____

_____

_____

_____

_____

_____

_____

_____

Name and Address

Memory

Name and Address

Memory

Name and Address

Memory

_____

_____

_____

_____

_____

_____

_____

_____

_____

_____

_____

_____

_____

_____

Name and Address

Memory

Name and Address

Memory

Name and Address

Memory

_____

_____

_____

_____

_____

_____

_____

_____

_____

_____

_____

_____

Name and Address

Memory

Name and Address

Memory

Name and Address

Memory

Name and Address

_____

_____

_____

_____

_____

_____

Memory

_____

_____

_____

_____

_____

_____

_____

_____

_____

Name and Address

_____

_____

_____

_____

_____

_____

Memory

_____

_____

_____

_____

_____

_____

_____

_____

_____

_____

_____

_____

Made in the USA
Monee, IL
06 July 2022